SCHOLASTIC

FILL-IN FLIP BOOKS

FOR GRAMMAR, VOCABULARY, AND MORE

by Michael Gravois

New York • Toronto • London • Auckland • Sydney

Mexico City • New Delhi • Hong Kong • Buenos Aires

Teaching Resources

DEDICATION

To Terry Cooper, Virginia Dooley, Mela Ottaiano, Sarah Longhi, Maria Chang,
and everyone at Scholastic Teaching Resources—
What a pleasure it is to work with you.
Thanks for your faith and support throughout the years.

Cover design by Adana Jiménez
Interior design by Michael Gravois
Interior illustrations by Jim Palmer and Amanda Haley
Photo page 63 © Kris Kuenning/National Science Foundation

ISBN 0-439-67682-7

Printed in the U.S.A.

1 2 3 4 5 6 7 8 9 10   40   12 11 10 09 08 07 06 05

CONTENTS

INTRODUCTION

"Tell me and I will forget. Show me and I will remember. Involve me and I will understand." Aristotle said this more than 2,300 years ago, yet its echoes can be heard in the philosophies of many modern educational theorists. The activities in this book embrace this philosophy by allowing students to become active participants in their own learning, challenging them to discover, question, explore, and problem solve.

This book features 25 ready-to-go flip books that focus on the language arts skills of spelling, grammar, reading, and writing. These hands-on activities motivate reluctant writers, relate the language arts to real-world experiences, and improve higher-level thinking skills. As students construct and complete the flip books, they will employ a variety of intelligences and learning styles. But best of all, the flip books break the information down into digestible chunks, allowing students to fearlessly take ownership of their learning.

CREATING FLIP BOOKS

The activities in this book all use standard 8½" by 11" copier paper, but flip books can be made in many sizes and with a varying number of pages. Once you get the hang of it, try making your own flip books using legal-size paper, construction paper, or even large strips of bulletin board paper.

On page 5 you will find directions for creating the three styles of flip books that this book uses. The individual activities are listed on pages 6–12. Underneath each listing is a description of the activity, the template pages you will need to copy, and a reference to which style's directions you need to follow to create the corresponding flip book.

NOTE

When you use this book, I urge you to first look over the list of activities on pages 6–12. Find a topic that interests you, and follow the directions for constructing it. Simply flipping through the template pages before actually constructing the flip book may confuse you because the tops and bottoms of each panel—as seen on the template—don't relate to each other. It is only *after* the flip books are assembled that the top and bottom panels correspond.

FLIP BOOK STYLE #1 uses one sheet of paper cut in half horizontally.

1. Copy the templates back-to-back (panel 2 on the back page should be upside down, behind panel 1). Have students cut along the dotted line to create two panels (figure 1, below).

2. Have students place the panels on top of one another, overlapping them so that the title strip of panel 1 shows below the cover panel (figure 2).

3. Ask students to fold the tops of the panels backward—panels 2 and 3 should show below panel 1 (figure 3). The top can be fastened with two staples (figure 4).

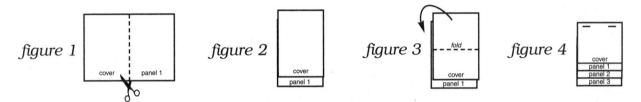

FLIP BOOK STYLE #2 uses one sheet of paper cut in half twice horizontally.

1. Copy the templates back-to-back (panel 5 on the back page should be upside down, behind the cover panel). Have students cut along the dotted lines to create three panels (figure 1, below).

2. Have students place the panels on top of one another, overlapping them (figure 2).

3. Ask students to fold the tops of the panels backward—panels 3, 4, and 5 should show below panel 2 (figure 3). The top can be fastened with two staples (figure 4).

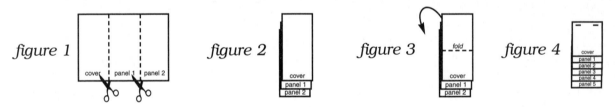

FLIP BOOK STYLE #3 uses two sheets of paper cut in half vertically.

1. Copy the templates back-to-back (the sheet with panels 6 and 7 should be upside down on the side behind the cover panel and panel 1; the sheet with panels 4 and 5 should be upside down on the side behind panels 2 and 3). Have students cut along the dotted lines to create four panels (figure 1, below).

2. Have students place the panels on top of one another, overlapping them so that the title strips of the cover panel and panels 1, 2, and 3 are offset from each other (figure 2).

3. Ask students to fold the tops of the panels backward—panels 4, 5, 6, and 7 should show below panel 3 (figure 3). The top can be fastened with two staples (figure 4).

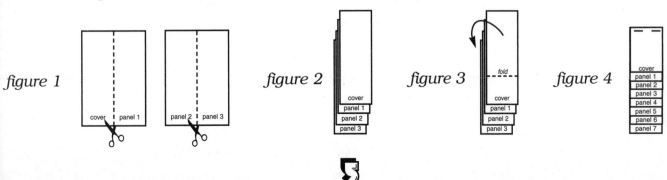

GRAMMAR ACTIVITIES

Mark My Words!—Punctuation Marks

Punctuate learning with this how-to guide that teaches the ins and outs of four basic punctuation marks—exclamation points, question marks, periods, and commas. After students complete the flip book, they can keep it as a handy reference guide to use throughout the year.

Copy the templates on pages 13–14 back to back (panel 5 on the back page should be opposite the cover). Use the instructions for Flip Book Style #2 on page 5 to construct this flip book.

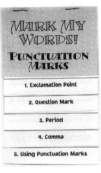

Studying Sentences

Challenge students to complete puzzles and play games that teach them about the four kinds of sentences, ending punctuation, and subjects and predicates.

Copy the templates on pages 15–16 back to back (panel 5 on the back page should be opposite the cover). Use the instructions for Flip Book Style #2 on page 5 to construct this flip book.

My Flip Book of Nouns

Use this flip book as a teaching tool and a study guide. Fill it out as a class and discuss the differences between common and proper nouns and the rules for changing singular nouns to plural nouns. Then, students can refer to their flip book when they study for a related test.

Copy the templates on pages 17–18 back to back (panel 2 on the back page should be opposite panel 1). Use the instructions for Flip Book Style #1 on page 5 to construct this flip book.

Don't Be Tense—Working With Verbs

Choosing the correct verb helps writers paint clearer, more precise pictures in the reader's mind. This flip book helps students understand this concept and gives them more experience in applying the use of past, present, and future tenses of verbs.

Copy the templates on pages 19–20 back to back (panel 5 on the back page should be opposite the cover). Use the instructions for Flip Book Style #2 on page 5 to construct this flip book.

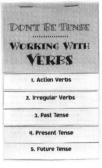

All About Adjectives

Think how bland writing would be without adjectives. They add spice and color to writing, allowing the writer to describe a specific person, place, thing, or idea. Students use their imagination to complete this flip book as they carefully select adjectives to describe themselves and the world around them.

Copy the templates on pages 21–22 back to back (panel 5 on the back page should be opposite the cover). Use the instructions for Flip Book Style #2 on page 5 to construct this flip book.

Writing With Adverbs

Add a dash of fun to your classroom by using wordplay and creative dramatics to teach the descriptive power of adverbs. However, remind students to avoid overusing adverbs. Discuss the value of choosing a strong verb, which often eliminates the need for adverbs. For example, rather than writing *She walked angrily out of the room*, you could simply write *She stormed out of the room*.

To play the adverb game that is discussed on panel 4 of this flip book, cut some white paper into a bunch of strips. Write an adverb on each strip. Put the strips into a jar. Ask a student to pull a strip of paper from the jar and walk across the front of the room in the manner that the adverb suggests. For example, if the adverb selected is *sadly*, the student could walk across the room slowly, with downcast eyes, sniffling, and wiping his eyes. The other students should write the adverb on the first line of panel four. After all of the students have had a chance to perform, find out what the actual adverbs were. Which student got the most correct? (Suggested adverbs include *sadly, joyfully, angrily, quietly, loudly, clumsily, quickly, slowly, shyly, bravely, cowardly, robotically, smoothly, mischievously, sneakily, sleepily, ordinarily*, and so on.)

Copy the templates on pages 23–24 back to back (panel 5 on the back page should be opposite the cover). Use the instructions for Flip Book Style #2 on page 5 to construct this flip book.

VOCABULARY ACTIVITIES

Spelling Partners

Have students work in pairs to create spelling puzzles for each other to solve. This two-person flip book challenges students to unscramble spelling words and learn their definitions, find synonyms, solve word search puzzles, and learn to identify spelling words as used in the context of a story.

Copy the templates on pages 25–26 back to back (panel 5 on the back page should be opposite the cover). Use the instructions for Flip Book Style #2 on page 5 to construct this flip book.

Learning New Vocabulary

Help students retain new vocabulary words by asking them to explore the words in greater detail—finding their definitions, recording their synonyms and antonyms, using them in sentences, and drawing simple pictures.

Copy the templates on pages 27–28 back to back (panel 5 on the back page should be opposite the cover). Use the instructions for Flip Book Style #2 on page 5 to construct this flip book.

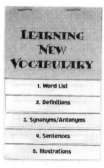

Synonyms and Antonyms

Use song lyrics, nursery rhymes, poetry, and autobiographies to help develop students' understanding of synonyms and antonyms. Allow students to use a thesaurus as they complete this flip book to help them find just the right words.

Copy the templates on pages 29–30 back to back (panel 5 on the back page should be opposite the cover). Use the instructions for Flip Book Style #2 on page 5 to construct this flip book.

Fooling Around With Compounds

There are thousands of compound words that come in three basic forms, and the degree to which you explore these unique words is for you to determine. This flip book introduces students to the three basic forms of compound words and provides a selected list of these words. But more important, it focuses on the fun you can have with wordplay.

Copy the templates on pages 31–32 back to back (panel 5 on the back page should be opposite the cover). Use the instructions for Flip Book Style #2 on page 5 to construct this flip book.

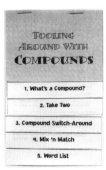

Homophones—Witch Word Is Write?

Homophones are quirky words that allow students to have fun with language. Imagine Rapunzel letting down her hare or Cinderella going to a bawl. Use this flip book to teach the concept of homophones, and then—as a follow-up activity—have students create art that illustrates the misuse of homophones. Hang the art on a bulletin board.

Copy the templates on pages 33–34 back to back (panel 5 on the back page should be opposite the cover). Use the instructions for Flip Book Style #2 on page 5 to construct this flip book.

Homonyms—Exploring Multiple Meanings of the Same Word

Homonyms are close cousins of homophones, having a slight—but important—difference. Homophones are words that are pronounced alike but have different spellings and meanings (*their, there*), while homonyms are words that are spelled *and* pronounced alike but differ in meaning (a swimming *pool*, a *pool* table, and to *pool* resources). Challenge students to come up with as many meanings as possible for these homonyms—*play, plant, snap, date, change, post, cool,* and *drive.*

Copy the templates on pages 35–36 back to back (panel 5 on the back page should be opposite the cover). Use the instructions for Flip Book Style #2 on page 5 to construct this flip book.

Studying Idioms—A Flip Book of the Five Senses

Idioms help students understand metaphors and find the relationships between language and life experience. This "Five Senses Flip Book" was taken from *20 Hands-On Activities for Learning Idioms* by Michael Gravois (Scholastic, 2002). Another great resource is the *Scholastic Dictionary of Idioms* by Marvin Terban (Scholastic, 1996).

Copy the templates on pages 37–38 back to back (panel 5 on the back page should be opposite the cover). Use the instructions for Flip Book Style #2 on page 5 to construct this flip book.

Foreign Words and Phrases

Explore the world through language by introducing students to commonly used foreign words and phrases. Students learn basic greetings in five foreign languages and have the opportunity to explore a language of their choice. The flip book also familiarizes students with common phrases they might come across in their reading or hear in everyday conversation.

Copy the templates on pages 39–40 back to back (panel 5 on the back page should be opposite the cover). Use the instructions for Flip Book Style #2 on page 5 to construct this flip book.

READING AND WRITING ACTIVITIES

Story Elements Book Report

Little Miss Muffet (*protagonist*) sat on a tuffet (*setting*) eating her curds and whey (*plot*). Along came a spider (*antagonist*) and sat down beside her (*problem*) and frightened Miss Muffet away (*solution*). Using this clever device, students learn about the main elements of a story, relate them to a novel they read, and create a flip book that shows their understanding.

    Copy the templates on pages 41–44 back to back (panel 1 should be directly behind panel 6; panel 2 should be directly behind panel 5). Use the instructions for Flip Book Style #3 on page 5 to construct this flip book. Ask students to write the title of their book, the author's name, and their own name on the cover of this flip book.

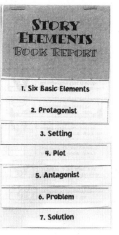

What a Character!

Readers learn about characters through the actions the character performs and through dialogue—what others say about the character and what the character says about himself or herself. Ask students to spend time with the main character of a novel they read to learn ways the author reveals the character's traits, strengths, and weaknesses.

    Copy the templates on pages 45–48 back to back (panel 1 should be directly behind panel 6; panel 2 should be directly behind panel 5). Use the instructions for Flip Book Style #3 on page 5 to construct this flip book.

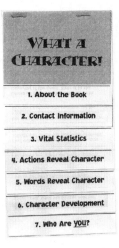

A Biography of...

After researching or reading a biography of a person they admire, students can record their findings in this flip book. Not only do students record factual information about the person's life and accomplishments, but they use higher-level thinking skills as they compare themselves to the person they studied and answer "interview" questions from the subject's point of view.

    Copy the templates on pages 49–50 back to back (panel 5 on the back page should be opposite the cover). Use the instructions for Flip Book Style #2 on page 5 to construct this flip book.

My Fantastic Flip Book of Figurative Language

Good writing can make words dance on your tongue or paint surprising pictures in your head. Get your students to think about how to best "turn a phrase" by exposing them to seven forms of figurative language—consonance, assonance, alliteration, onomatopoeia, simile, metaphor, and personification.

Copy the templates on pages 51–54 back to back (panel 1 should be directly behind panel 6; panel 2 should be directly behind panel 5). Use the instructions for Flip Book Style #3 on page 5 to construct this flip book.

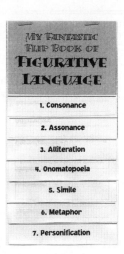

Improving My Writing

Three ready-to-go graphic organizers help students improve word choice, develop more vivid characters, and construct more elaborate sentences—teaching them strategies they can use in their writing for years to come.

Copy the templates on pages 55–56 back to back (panel 2 on the back page should be opposite panel 1). Use the instructions for Flip Book Style #1 on page 5 to construct this flip book.

I'm a Poet! And I Know It!

Create a classroom of poets by having students study the seven types of poems featured in this flip book—couplets, alphabet poems, haiku, quatrains, cinquains, limericks, and shape poems. Each panel contains descriptions of the poetic style and space for students to write their own poems.

Copy the templates on pages 57–60 back to back (panel 1 should be directly behind panel 6; panel 2 should be directly behind panel 5). Use the instructions for Flip Book Style #3 on page 5 to construct this flip book.

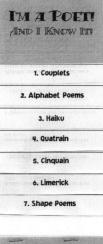

"Just the Facts, Ma'am"—Newspaper Reporting

Students "get to the meat of the matter" as they learn about reporting techniques—the inverted pyramid style of reporting, writing headlines and captions, and the 5Ws. They develop higher-level thinking skills by exploring the concept of *freedom of the press*. And finally, students put their understanding of these concepts to the test by writing articles about real-life experiences and events.

Copy the templates on pages 61–64 back to back (panel 1 should be directly behind panel 6; panel 2 should be directly behind panel 5). Use the instructions for Flip Book Style #3 on page 5 to construct this flip book.

Editing and Proofreading—Reference Guide

This handy reference guide offers proofreading tips, a proof-reading checklist, and a chart of proofreading marks. Students can keep this flip book close at hand throughout the year, allowing them to use the vocabulary of an editor as they revise their writing.

Copy the templates on pages 65–66 back to back (panel 2 on the back page should be opposite panel 1). Use the instructions for Flip Book Style #1 on page 5 to construct this flip book.

Reading Response Log

A reading response log is a record of a reader's thoughts, ideas, feelings, reactions, observations, and questions he or she might have while reading a book. As students read a novel, allow them to jump between the panels of this flip book, responding to the prompts as they are inspired. Or you might want to assign panels you feel best relate to certain sections in the book.

Copy the templates on pages 67–70 back to back (panel 1 should be directly behind panel 6; panel 2 should be directly behind panel 5). Use the instructions for Flip Book Style #3 on page 5 to construct this flip book.

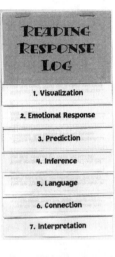

My Weekly Journal

Seven interesting writing prompts spark students' creativity in this journaling flip book. Use the ideas in this flip book as warmups at the beginning of your writing class. It is also a great homework activity for students to complete at their own pace over the course of a week—seven panels, seven prompts, one for each day of the week. Use the blank journaling template, as explained in the next section, to create your own prompts for students.

Copy the templates on pages 71–74 back to back (panel 1 should be directly behind panel 6; panel 2 should be directly behind panel 5). Use the instructions for Flip Book Style #3 on page 5 to construct this flip book.

My Weekly Journal (blank template)

Design a customized Weekly Journal featuring writing prompts that you create. First, construct a flip book using the blank templates on pages 75–78. Next, write your prompts in the empty space at the top of each panel. Then, disassemble the flip book, lay the pages side by side, and copy the pages on a copier machine. Finally, pass out the pages for your students to assemble and complete.

Copy the templates on pages 75–78 back to back (panel 1 should be directly behind panel 6; panel 2 should be directly behind panel 5). Use the instructions for Flip Book Style #3 on page 5 to construct this flip book.

Commas are tricky little marks with a lot of rules. They can be used like short rest stops in writing or to keep words and ideas from running together.

Use commas—

1) to separate three or more items in a series.

   Tom, Dick, and Harry like to hop, skip, and jump.

2) to separate two independent clauses.

   Tom likes to hop, but Harry likes to jump.

3) to to set off introductory phrases.

   Jumping with excitement, Tom claimed his prize.

4) to set off appositives (added information).

   Tom and Dick, my twin brothers, like to play hopscotch.

5) to separate adjectives.

   The quarterback threw a long, accurate pass.

2. Question Mark

All of the punctuation has been removed from the following passage. Use a colored pen or pencil to add exclamation points, question marks, periods, and commas.

Dear Ms Lucker

On May 4 2004 we met at a conference in Des Moines Iowa I gave a speech on environmental awareness and you were on the panel discussing global warming Do you remember me I am conducting a seminar next October in Buffalo New York and I would like for you to be a guest speaker Please say you'll come You

Draw a cartoon that features a character saying something loudly. Use an exclamation point.

1. Exclamation Point

MARK MY WORDS:
PUNCTUATION MARKS

The smallest punctuation mark, a **period**, is also one of the most useful and most used. Sometimes it's called a **full stop**.

Use a period—

1) after a sentence that makes a statement.
   We're going to the zoo.
2) after a sentence that gives a command.
   Come to the zoo with me.
3) after an initial.
   Susan B. Anthony
4) after abbreviations.
   Mr.   Mrs.   Ms.   Dr.   Washington, D.C.
5) as a decimal point.
   John's temperature was 101.3 degrees.
6) to separate dollars and cents.
   I spent $16.23 at the market today.

Write a few sentences on the lines below that use periods in a few of the ways described above.

_____

_____

_____

_____

When do you use a **question mark**? You use it after a direct question, of course!

   Have you ever been to California?

But *don't* put a question mark after an indirect question.

   He asked the boy if he had ever been to California.

Carry this flip book around with you today. Listen carefully to everyday conversations that people have. On the lines below, write a few of the questions you overhear.

---

6) in dates.
   July 4, 1776
7) to separate cities and states.
   New Orleans, Louisiana
8) to make numbers easier to read.
   1,348,622
9) to set off quoted phrases.
   "Use a comma here," said the teacher.
10) in direct address.
   Tom, have you seen Harry?
11) After the salutation and closing of a letter.
   Dear Tom, (salutation)
   Sincerely, (closing)
12) to set off an interjection from the rest of a sentence.
   Wow, that's a beautiful necklace!

The **exclamation point** is like writing with a volume control. Use it at the end of a sentence to show you *really, really* mean it.

   Don't make me tell you again!

Or use it at the end of a single word to make the word seem louder.

   Help! Fire!

---

will receive a payment of $3500 for your services but we are unable to offer you travel expenses

Ms Lucker you would be an engaging inspiring speaker to have at our seminar I hope you strongly consider accepting my offer Are you available in October Boy Are you even interested Boy we sure would love for you to attend

Call me at your earliest convenience

Sincerely
Mrs Stephanie I Badinger

Underline the simple subject in each sentence. Then write each simple subject in the spaces below. The boxed letters, reading down, will complete this sentence: When the T-Rex stubbed his toe, he became a _____.

1. Our new garden attracts colorful butterflies.

2. The piano on the stage needs tuning.

3. This island was a volcano many years ago.

4. Nobody knew the answer to the question.

5. My father's glasses broke yesterday.

6. My sweet, friendly dog scares people because he's so large.

7. The girl with the red pom-poms is my sister.

I picked up the phone and applied ☐ And guess what ☐

They accepted my application ☐

I can't believe I'm going to do this ☐ My bags are packed, and the taxi is waiting ☐

Will I make it through the night ☐

2. Sentence Identification

Underline the simple predicate in each sentence. Then find and circle the simple predicate in the word search puzzle below.

1. Kyle plays the trumpet in the school band.

2. The band marched at halftime during the football game.

3. The captain of the football team scored three touchdowns in the fourth quarter!

4. Andy Perry, the school's principal, announced the final score over the loudspeaker.

5. The rowdy crowd of students cheered loudly for the winning team.

6. The coach praised his players for their strong performance.

7. The bus transported the band back to school.

8. The exhausted players slept soundly that night.

An **imperative sentence** gives a command and ends with a period.

An **exclamatory sentence** expresses excitement and ends with an exclamation point.

1. Kinds of Sentences

STUDYING SENTENCES

A **declarative sentence** makes a statement and ends with a period.

An **interrogative sentence** asks a question and ends with a question mark.

A	B	P	L	A	Y	S	N	G
P	T	A	Y	E	R	W	I	N
C	R	L	S	R	F	U	C	S
A	A	O	C	L	A	L	H	T
A	N	O	U	N	C	E	D	
P	S	P	R	A	I	S	E	D
S	P	O	E	K	O	L	R	E
L	O	H	D	Y	U	E	E	R
E	R	C	H	E	E	P	D	O
P	T	E	C	M	R	T	P	P
P	E	D	L	M	S	S	E	O
T	D	M	A	R	C	H	E	D

Write the correct ending punctuation marks in the boxes below.

Are you brave enough ☐ That's what the ad said ☐ It challenged someone to spend the night in a haunted house ☐

Jake dared me, "Answer the ad, Charlie ☐ "

8. The houses in this neighborhood were built over one hundred years ago.

1.
2.
3.
4.
5.
6.
7.
8.

Work in groups of four. First, write a declarative sentence on the lines below.

_____

_____

Next, pass the flip book to a group member and have him or her change the sentence into an interrogative one.

_____

_____

Then, have the third group member change the sentence to an imperative one.

_____

_____

Then, have the fourth group member change it to an exclamatory sentence.

_____

_____

Finally, check to see that the sentences are written and punctuated correctly.

Rules for Forming Plural Nouns

Write the correct plural form of each noun in the box below the rule.

1. To change most nouns from singular to plural, just add -s.

singular	plural	singular	plural
teacher		girl	

2. Add -es to nouns that end in s, ss, sh, ch, x, or z.

singular	plural	singular	plural
bush		dress	
bench		fox	

3. If a noun ends in a consonant + y, change the y to i and add -es.

singular	plural	singular	plural
baby		country	

Noun Hunt

Circle the 19 common and proper nouns in the following passage.

On Tuesday, our class took a trip to the Metropolitan Museum of Art in New York City. We saw artwork and sculptures by many artists. I really liked the paintings by Pablo Picasso because he used bright colors and interesting shapes. After three hours of walking through the museum, we ate lunch in the cafeteria. Then we got on the bus and returned to school. What a fun day!

1. Common & Proper Nouns

On the front cover of your flip book, write your name and draw three simple icons representing a person, a place, and a thing.

MY FLIP BOOK OF NOUNS

Rules for Capitalizing Proper Nouns

1. Capitalize the first letter in the names of people and pets (first *and* last names).

(examples: Benjamin Franklin, Fido, Mr. and Mrs. Chin, Batman)

2. Capitalize the names of particular places and things, except for little words like *of*, *the*, or *by*.

(examples: the United States of America, Fifth Avenue, San Diego, the Gulf of Mexico, *Charlotte's Web*)

3. Capitalize the names of months, days, and holidays, except for little words like *of*, *the*, or *by*.

(examples: February, Wednesday, the Fourth of July.)

Capital Capers

Circle the letters in the following passage that should be capitalized. You should find 22 missing capital letters in all.

"Our dog has been missing since last saturday," cried anne. "His name is mr. bojangles, and he has white fur with a black spot around his eyes. He ran away from smith's grocery on marigold drive."

The veterinarian, doctor ling, looked at the sad girl and said, "mayor andrew lund brought a lost dog here on monday. Perhaps it's mr. bojangles."

doctor ling and anne went into the holding pen. Suddenly a little white dog started barking.

"mr. bojangles!" exclaimed anne. She hugged the little dog as if she'd never let go.

2. Capitalization

A *common noun* names a general person, place, or thing.
A *proper noun* names a particular person, place, or thing.

common	proper	common	proper
president	John Adams	country	Canada

Fill in the chart below with other examples of common and proper people, places, and things.

common	proper	common	proper

4. When a noun ends in a vowel + *y*, just add -s.

singular	plural	singular	plural
monkey		boy	

5. For nouns that end in *f* or *fe*, change the *f* to *v* and add -*es* or -*s* (exceptions: roofs, chiefs).

singular	plural	singular	plural
knife		wolf	

6. Some nouns change their spelling to form the plural.

singular	plural	singular	plural
child		woman	
foot		goose	

7. Some nouns remain the same for both singular and plural.

singular	plural	singular	plural
moose		deer	
salmon		sheep	

3. Singular & Plural Nouns

Use the same topic you wrote about on panel 3 and write another paragraph using present tense verbs—for example: *The petunias are bursting with color and cause people to stop and enjoy their beauty.*

1.
2.
3.
4.
5.
6.
7.
8.

Using the same topic, write another paragraph using future tense verbs—for example: *In the fall the leaves will turn brown and the frost will kill my beautiful petunias.*

WALK

DON'T BE TENSE

WORKING WITH VERBS

Improve your writing by choosing the right verb. How does the image of someone walking home change based on the verbs in the following three sentences? I walked home. I hobbled home. I skipped home.

Come up with ten different verbs that could be used instead of *walk* to make your writing clearer. Use a thesaurus if necessary.

To change most verbs to the past tense you simply add -ed to the end. Verbs that do not follow this rule are called **irregular verbs.** Write the past tense of each verb in the spaces below. The boxed letters, reading down, will complete this pun: When spring finally arrived the maple tree said, "I'm so _____."

1. bring
2. go
3. fly
4. eat

5. catch
6. dive
7. wear
8. do

Pick a topic and write a paragraph about it using past tense verbs—for example: *Last spring I planted petunias around the tree and watered them daily.*

3. Past Tense

4. Present Tense

5. Future Tense

Adjective Acrostics use each letter of a word as the first letter of an adjective that describes the word.

F earless
I ntense
R eliable
E nergetic
M uscular
A thletic
N oble

Write a paragraph about something you like. Use "positive" adjectives—such as *exciting* or *beautiful*—to support your opinion.

_____

_____

_____

_____

_____

_____

_____

_____

2. "Around Me" Adjectives

1. "About Me" Adjectives

ALL ABOUT ADJECTIVES

Draw a picture of one of your favorite foods.

Name ten nouns you can find in your classroom. Use an adjective to describe each one.

ADJECTIVE **NOUN**

Write a description of the food that might be found on a menu. Use adjectives that describe the look, taste, and smell of the food.

Write your name in the oval. Then write eight adjectives that describe your personality and/or your appearance.

Write a paragraph about something you dislike. Use "negative" adjectives—such as *wicked* or *boring*—to support your opinion.

Choose an occupation and write an adjective acrostic for it. Draw a related illustration.

3. Appetizing Adjectives

4. Working With Adjectives

5. Persuasive Adjectives

WRITING WITH ADVERBS

In this creative dramatics game, each class member will walk across the room in a way that expresses a "how" adverb (sadly, loudly, clumsily, etc.). Try to guess the adverb your friends are acting out. Write the adverbs below. Check the box in front of the adverbs you guessed correctly.

☐ _____

☐ _____

☐ _____

☐ _____

☐ _____

☐ _____

---

the show is over, my little brother gets _____ sad, and my mother _____ comforts him. I hope we can go to the circus again _____ . What a(n) _____ fun day!

soon	happily	gently
really	incredibly	wildly
very	magically	especially

2. Practice

A **Tom Swifty** is a form of wordplay where an adverb is used as a pun to describe how something is being said—for example:

"Who turned off the lights?" Tom asked darkly.

"This pencil needs to be sharpened," Tom said bluntly.

"The doctor removed my left ventrical," cried Tom half-heartedly.

Choose adverbs from the box below to complete these Tom Swiftys:

"It's time to go to the cemetery," Tom said _____ .

"The house is on fire!" yelled Tom _____ .

"I like to go camping," Tom said _____ .

When? She mailed it *yesterday.* (or *today, immediately, soon,* etc.)

How often? She *always* writes letters. (or *often, never, rarely,* etc.)

To what extent? She writes *very* neatly. (or *too, so, really,* etc.)

1. What's an Adverb?

An **adverb** is a word that describes a verb, an adjective, or another adverb. It tells how, where, when, how often, and to what extent.

How? She wrote *neatly*.
(or *happily, quietly, quickly,* etc.)

Where? The envelope was *nearby*.
(or *there, here, somewhere,* etc.)

Choose adverbs from the box below—or come up with your own—to make the following passage more descriptive and interesting.

We _____ like to go to the circus. We _____ like the clowns. They _____ appear from a little car and laugh _____ when they get hit with pies. The crowd _____ applauds. When

---

Brainstorm adverbs that tell *when* or *how often*. Use the sentences below to help you.

John _____ wants to go to bed

John wants to go to bed _____

WHEN Adverbs

rarely

now

Brainstorm adverbs that tell *where*. Use the sentence below to help you.

John runs _____ .

WHERE Adverbs

everywhere

outside

there

3. Adverbs Tell When & Where

4. Adverbs Tell How

5. Tom Swiftys

"I'm so embarrassed," Tom said _____.

"The earth is *not flat*," Tom said _____

"I have absolutely no idea," Tom said _____.

roundly   intently   gravely
alarmingly   readily   thoughtlessly

Write your own Tom Swifty below.

Partner 1: Use eight of your spelling words to create a story on the lines below, but leave a blank where the spelling word belongs.

Partner 2: Use eight of your spelling words to fill in the blanks below and complete the story.

1. Scrambled Spelling

Partner 1: Create a word search using eight of your spelling words. Write the eight words on the lines below.

Partner 2: Find the eight words hidden in the word search puzzle. Shade in the boxes that contain the letters of your spelling words.

1.
2.
3.
4.
5.
6.
7.
8.

2. Reverse Dictionary

SPELLING PARTNERS

PARTNER 1: _____

PARTNER 2: _____

Partner 1: Look up three spelling words in a thesaurus. Write several synonyms for each word in the large boxes below.
Partner 2: Look at the synonyms below and figure out which spelling words they describe. Write the spelling word in the small box above each list.

Partner 1: Write the definitions of three spelling words on the lines below each box.
Partner 2: Write the spelling word in the box that the definition below it describes.

Partner 1: Write the scrambled letters of three spelling words on the lines below each box.
Partner 2: Unscramble the letters below to reveal three spelling words. Write the word in the box above the scrambled letters.

3. Thesaurus

4. Word Search

5. Context Clues

Write words 5 and 6 below. Then write their definitions. Use each word in a sentence that conveys its meaning.

Word: _____

Definition: _____

_____

_____

_____

Sentence: _____

_____

_____

Word: _____

Definition: _____

_____

_____

2. Definitions

Write words 7 and 8 below. Then write their definitions and draw a simple picture to help you remember the meaning of the words.

Word: _____

Definition: _____

_____

_____

4. _____

5. _____

6. _____

7. _____

8. _____

1. Word List

LEARNING NEW VOCABULARY

Write your eight vocabulary words below. Order them, starting with the one you think will be easiest to learn, and ending with the one you think will be hardest.

1. _____

2. _____

3. _____

Write words 1 and 2 below. Then write their definitions in the space provided.

Word: _____

Definition: _____
_____
_____
_____

Word: _____

Definition: _____
_____
_____
_____

Write words 3 and 4 below. Then write their definitions, followed by a synonym and antonym for each.

Word: _____

Definition: _____
_____
_____
_____

Synonym: _____

Antonym: _____

Word: _____

Definition: _____
_____
_____
_____

Synonym: _____

Antonym: _____

Word: _____

Definition: _____
_____
_____

Sentence: _____
_____
_____
_____

3. Synonyms/Antonyms

4. Sentences

5. Illustrations

SYNONYMS AND ANTONYMS

2. Synonym Poetry

Pick a short song and rewrite it using as many synonyms for the original words as possible.

Example:

OLD Twinkle, twinkle, little star,
NEW Glimmer, shimmer, tiny star,
OLD How I wonder what you are.
NEW How I question what you are.
OLD Up above the world so high,
NEW High over the earth so aloft,
OLD Like a diamond in the sky.
NEW Like a jewel in the heavens.
OLD Twinkle, twinkle, little star,
NEW Sparkle, glitter, puny star,
OLD How I wonder what you are.
NEW How I puzzle over what you are.

Write your own **synonym poem** below.

_____

_____

1. Anti-autobiographies

Circle the antonyms for these five words in the word search puzzle below. Write the antonyms next to each word. Use a thesaurus if necessary.

thaw _____

above _____

professional _____

ignite _____

yell _____

Circle the synonyms for these five words in the word search puzzle below. Write the synonyms next to each word. Use a thesaurus if necessary.

merrily _____

gentle _____

money _____

difficult _____

ask _____

Write a brief autobiography of yourself—but with a twist. Describe yourself with antonyms. For example, if you're a young boy who lives in a large city, you might say *I am an old man who lives in the country.*

A **synonym poem** is a three-line poem that follows these rules:

Line 1	—	Word
Line 2	—	3-5 synonyms of the word
Line 3	—	A phrase related to the word
	—	Lines 2 and 3 should rhyme.

Magicians
Conjurers, illusionists, prestidigitators
They never cease to amaze the spectators.

Pick a short nursery rhyme and rewrite it using as many antonyms as possible for the original words as possible.

Example:

OLD Wee Willie Winkie runs through the town,
NEW **Huge Willie Winkie walks around the countryside,**

OLD Upstairs and downstairs in his nightgown,
NEW **Downstairs and upstairs in his day pants,**

OLD Tapping at the window and crying through the lock,
NEW **Pounding at the window and laughing through the lock,**

OLD Are all the children in their beds, it's past eight o'clock?
NEW **Are all the adults in their chairs, it's before eight o'clock?**

3. Antonym Nursery Rhymes

4. Synonym Songs

5. Antonym/Synonym Search

A	B	P	Y	I	Y	S	N	G
A	C	B	E	N	E	A	T	H
M	R	L	H	G	F	U	E	S
A	J	O	C	U	A	L	X	T
T	O	B	E	I	E	A	T	E
E	Y	P	T	R	O	S	I	H
U	F	R	E	E	Z	E	N	A
R	U	H	N	Y	U	E	G	R
E	L	C	D	E	L	B	U	D
T	L	T	E	N	G	T	I	L
F	Y	D	R	M	C	A	S	H
W	H	I	S	P	E	R	H	D

1. Pick two compound words. Write them on the lines below.

Example: bedroom, candlestick

_____

_____

2. Switch the first halves of the two words to create two new compound words. Write them on the lines below.

Example: bedstick, candleroom

_____

_____

3. Define the new compound words and use each of them in a sentence.

Example: A bedstick is a long rod used to beat bedbugs out of mattresses.

3. Write a definition for the new compound word on the lines below.

Example: A chairbrush is a sticky brush used to take lint and pet hair off your furniture.

2. Take Two

There are hundreds of *closed-form* compound words. Here's an alphabetical list of some of them.

afternoon, afterthought, airmail, airplane, airport, another, anybody, anyone, anything, anywhere, armchair, babysitter, backboard, backbone, backpack, backspace, bandstand, baseball, basketball, bathroom, bathtub, battlefield, bedroom, bedtime, bellbottom, birdhouse, birthday, blackberry, blackboard, bluebird, bookcase, boyfriend, breakfast, campfire, candlestick, cardboard, carsick, chairman, classmate, clockwork, cowboy, crossword, cupboard, cupcake, darkroom, daylight, doghouse, doorbell, doorknob, downstairs, driveway, earring, evergreen, everyone, everything, eyeball, fingernail, fireman, fireplace, fishhook, flagpole, flashlight, football, footprint, footstep, gentleman, goldfish, grandmother, grasshopper, gumball, hairbrush, haircut, handbag, handwriting, headache, headdress, henhouse, highway, hilltop, himself, homework, horseback, hourglass, houseboat,

Hyphenated Form: The words are separated by a hyphen.

mother-in-law, merry-go-round, over-the-counter

Open Form: The words are written as separate words, but when used together have a singular meaning.

post office, ice cream, police car

1. What's a Compound?

FOOLING AROUND WITH COMPOUNDS

A **compound word** is a word formed by combining two or more words.

There are three forms of compound words.

Closed Form: The words are joined together to form a new word.

outside, bedroom, birthday, cupcake

1. Choose two short words and write them on the line below.

   Example: chair, brush

2. Join the two words together to make a new compound word. Write the new word on the line below.

   Example: chairbrush

1. Pick a compound word and write it on the line below.

   Example: airmail

2. Switch around the two halves of the word to create a new compound word.

   Example: mailair

3. Draw a picture of the new compound word in the box below and write its definition.

   Example: Mailair is the air that gets trapped inside envelopes and makes them puffy.

housekeeper, indoors, inside, keyboard, keyhole, ladybug, lampshade, landmark, landslide, lawnmower, lifeboat, lifeguard, lighthouse, mailbox, masterpiece, moonlight, motorcycle, newspaper, nightgown, nightmare, nobody, nothing, nutcracker, oatmeal, outhouse, outlaw, outside, overcoat, oversleep, pancake, paperback, pickup, pitchfork, playgoer, playground, popcorn, postmark, quicksand, railroad, rainbow, raincoat, roommate, rosebud, sailboat, salesperson, sandbox, sandpaper, scarecrow, schoolhouse, scoreboard, shoestring, shortcut, sidewalk, skateboard, skyline, skyscraper, snowflake, snowman, someone, somewhere, spaceship, starfish, streetcar, suitcase, sunburn, sunflower, sunlight, surfboard, sweetheart, teacup, teenage, textbook, thunderstorm, tiptoe, toadstool, toothbrush, toothpaste, typewriter, undertaker, underwear, update, uplift, upstairs, waistline, wallpaper, warehouse, waterfall, weekend, wherever, whirlpool, windpipe, yearbook, zookeeper

3. Compound Switch-Around

4. Mix 'n Match

5. Word List

Here is a list of some homophone pairs. Search the Internet for others. There are many sites dedicated to these unique words.

aisle	isle	grate	great	know	no
arc	ark	hangar	hanger	lead	led
ate	eight	hare	hair	made	maid
ball	bawl	hay	hey	mail	male
bare	bear	heal	heel	main	mane
be	bee	hear	here	meat	meet
blew	blue	heard	herd	one	won
bough	bow	hi	high	pain	pane
brake	break	higher	hire	pair	pear
cell	sell	him	hymn	peace	piece
cheap	cheep	hole	whole	plane	plain
creak	creek	hour	our	pray	prey
dear	deer	idle	idol	rap	wrap
die	dye	in	inn	read	reed
fair	fare	knead	need	right	write
flour	flower	knew	new	road	rode
forth	fourth	knight	night	role	roll
foul	fowl	knot	not	root	route

Use the word list to write a story that contains as many homophones as possible. Highlight all the homophones in your story.

_____
_____
_____
_____
_____
_____
_____
_____
_____
_____
_____

2. Picture This

The word *homophone* comes from the Greek words *homo* (same) and *phonos* (sound).

1. What's a Homophone?

HOMOPHONES
....
WHICH WORD
IS WRITE?

Homophones
are words that
sound alike
but have different
meanings and spellings.

This limerick uses two pairs of homophones. Find and circle the homophones. Draw a picture in the box below to illustrate the limerick.

A flea and a fly in a flue
Were imprisoned, so what could they do?
   Said the flea, "Let us fly!"
   Said the fly, "Let us flee!"
So they flew through a flaw in the flue.

sale	sail	steal	steel	waist	waste
sea	see	sweet	suite	wait	weight
seas	seize	tale	tail	wear	where
seam	seem	team	teem	way	weigh
sole	soul	thyme	time	weak	week
some	sum	tide	tied	which	witch
son	sun	toe	tow	wood	would
stake	steak				

aye	eye	I	rain	reign	rein
buy	by	bye	raise	rays	raze
cent	scent	sent	sew	so	sow
dew	do	due	there	their	they're
ewe	yew	you	to	too	two
flew	flu	flue	vain	vane	vein
for	fore	four	way	weigh	whey
oar	or	ore			

Fill in the blanks with *weather* or *whether* to finish the poem.

The _____ is cold
Or _____ the _____ is hot,
We'll be together whatever the _____,
_____ we like it or not.

Circle the correct homophone in the following sentences:

1) Rapunzel, let down your **hair/hare.**

2) The baby **bare/bear** said, "Someone's been eating my porridge!"

3) King Midas had to be careful because he had a golden **cents/sense/scents** of touch.

4) The brave **knight/night** rescued Sleeping Beauty from the castle.

5) Little Miss Muffet sat on a tuffet eating her curds and **weigh/way/whey.**

6) The evil queen was very **vain/vane/vein.**

7) Chicken Little told all the other **foul/fowl** that the sky was falling.

8) Cinderella had to hurry if she was to get to the **ball/bawl.**

9) Three little kittens lost **they're/there/their** mittens, and they began **too/to/two** cry.

5. Story Thyme   **4. Word List**   **3. Picking Pairs/Pears**

In small groups, choose a homonym. Create three short scenes that use the word in different ways. Perform the scenes for the class. Write the word and a brief synopsis of each of your scenes below.

WORD

SCENE ONE

_____

_____

_____

_____

_____

6. The expert skier took the **run** at breakneck speed. (*an inclined course for skiing*)

7. While Mom went to the store we had the **run** of the house. (*freedom of movement*)

8. I can't talk now; I have to **run**. (*leave*)

9. The baseball team didn't make a single **run** the entire game. (*a score in baseball*)

10. I have to **run** to the store to get milk. (*go on an errand*)

2. Example

Record the homonyms that the other groups used in their scenes. After each homonym, write three short definitions that explain the different way the groups used each word.

_____

_____

_____

_____

_____

_____

The word *homonym* comes from the Greek words *homo* (same) and *nym* (name).

1. What's a Homonym?

HOMONYMS

Exploring Multiple Meanings of the Same Word

Homonyms
are words that are spelled
and pronounced alike but
are different in meaning.

RUN

1. When I am late I have to **run** for the bus. (*the act of running*)

2. My mother's fingernail snagged her stocking and caused a **run**. (*a rip*)

3. After winning ten games in a row, the team's **run** ended. (*a stretch of good or bad luck*)

4. Two brooks **run** through the woods near my house. (*flow*)

5. I put Rover in the dog **run** to get exercise. (*an animal enclosure*)

Brainstorm a list of homonyms. Write a different homonym in each box below. Using your own words, write two definitions for each homonym on the lines beneath the boxes.

SCENE TWO

SCENE THREE

3. Brainstorming

4. Acting Out

5. Look, Listen, and Learn

List three things that make you "down in the mouth."

1. _____

2. _____

3. _____

List three things that make you "foam at the mouth."

1. _____

2. _____

3. _____

Meanings of Hearing-Related Idioms

— young, inexperienced, and immature

— children often hear and understand a lot more than people give them credit for

— eager to listen; sharply attentive

— to create something valuable or beautiful out of something worthless or ugly

— to pay attention and become well-informed

2. Hearing

Idiom

Choose one of the idioms related to the sense of touch and circle it.

◆ **By the skin of your teeth**

◆ **Get under your skin**

◆ **No skin off your nose**

◆ **Touch and go**

◆ **Wouldn't touch something with a ten-foot pole**

Meaning

In your own words, write the meaning of the idiom you selected.

_____

_____

_____

_____

Draw a picture illustrating your description of something that is "a sight for sore eyes."

1. Sight

STUDYING IDIOMS
A FLIP BOOK
OF THE FIVE SENSES

Describe something that you would consider a "sight for sore eyes."

_____

_____

_____

Creative Writing
Write a short story that conveys the meaning of the idiom you selected.

_____

_____

_____

_____

_____

Write the number of each of the idioms from the list below on the line in front of its proper meaning.

1. All ears

2. Keep your ear to the ground

3. Little pitchers have big ears

4. Make a silk purse out of a sow's ear

5. Wet behind the ears

List three things that "make your mouth water."

1. _____

2. _____

3. _____

List three things that you like to "run off at the mouth" about.

1. _____

2. _____

3. _____

Fill in the blanks with the following idioms. Two idioms will not be used.

- ◆ **smell a rat**
- ◆ **come up smelling like a rose**
- ◆ **cut off your nose to spite your face**
- ◆ **pay through the nose**
- ◆ **follow your nose**
- ◆ **make it by a nose**
- ◆ **look down your nose at someone**

1. When a severe frost hits Florida, people have to _____ to buy orange juice.

2. You shouldn't _____ just because he or she looks different from you.

3. We're running a little late for the movie, but if we leave now we'll _____ .

4. "Even though you all claim to be innocent, I _____," said the detective.

5. When he asked me the way to the bakery, I said, "_____."

3. Smell

4. Taste

5. Touch

Write a conversation between two people that uses at least five common foreign phrases from the list on panel 5. Underline or highlight these phrases in your writing.

_____

_____

_____

_____

_____

_____

_____

2. Numbers

Five		
Six		
Seven		
Eight		
Nine		
Ten		

Read through this list of common foreign words and phrases. Check the box in front of any that you've heard before.

☐ **à la carte** (ah la kart') [Fr.] with a separate price for each item on the menu

☐ **à la mode** (ah la mohd') according to the prevailing style or fashion

☐ **aficionado** (uh fish' ya nah' doh) [Sp.] a devotee or fan

☐ **bon voyage** (bon' vwa-yazh') [Fr.] good journey

☐ **bona fide** (boh'na fide') [Lat.] authentic

☐ **carpe diem** (kar'pay dee'um) [Lat.] seize the day

☐ **carte blanche** (kart blonsh') [Fr.] unrestricted power to act on one's own

☐ **c'est la vie** (say' la vee) [Fr.] such is life

☐ **crème de la crème** (krem' de la krem') [Fr.] the best of the best

☐ **déjà vu** (day'zha voo') [Fr.] the mistaken impression of having seen or experienced something before

☐ **faux pas** (foh pah') [Fr.] a social blunder

☐ **glasnost** (glaz'nohst) [Rus.] a candid discussion of social problems

English	please	thank you
French	s'il vous plaît	merci
German	bitte	danke
Italian	per favore	grazie
Japanese	onegai-shimasu	arigatou
Spanish	por favor	gracias

English	yes	no
French	oui	non
German	ja	nein
Italian	si	no
Japanese	hai	iie
Spanish	si	no

1. Six Words/Six Languages

FOREIGN WORDS AND PHRASES

Pick a different language for each day of the school week and use as many of the words below as possible throughout the day.

English	hello	goodbye
French	bonjour	au revoir
German	hallo	auf Wiedersehen
Italian	ciao	arrivederci
Japanese	konnichiwa	sayonara
Spanish	hola	adiós

Research two foreign languages and write the words for the numbers 1 through 10 in the chart below.

English		
One		
Two		
Three		
Four		

Draw icons in the boxes below of six things that you would find in a classroom. Choose a foreign language and write the word for each object on the line under the appropriate box.

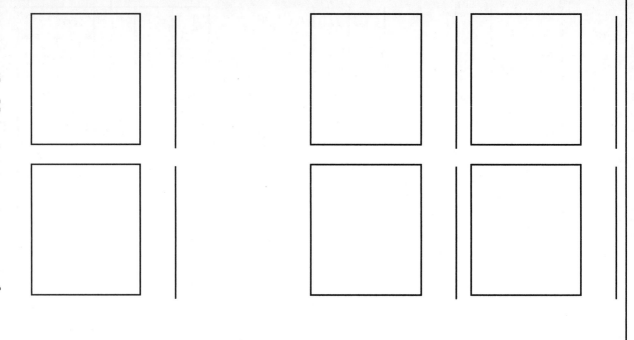

3. Around the Classroom

4. Writing With Foreign Phrases

5. Word and Phrase List

- ☐ **hoi polloi** (hoy' puh loy') [Gk.] the common people
- ☐ **hors d'oeuvre** (or derv') [Fr.] an appetizer served before a meal
- ☐ **joie de vivre** (zhwah' duh vee'vruh) [Fr.] carefree enjoyment of life
- ☐ **mano a mano** (mah'no ah mah'-no) [Sp.] a face-to-face confrontation or struggle
- ☐ **mea culpa** (may'uh kul'puh) [Lat.] an acknowledgment of personal blame
- ☐ **nom de plume** (nom duh ploom') [Fr.] pen name
- ☐ **non sequitur** (non sek'wi-ter) [Lat.] a statement that does not follow logically from what preceded it
- ☐ **répondez s'il vous plaît (r.s.v.p.)** (reh-pahn'-day seel voo pleh') [Fr.] please respond
- ☐ **shalom** (shah-lohm') [Heb.] a traditional Jewish greeting or farewell, peace
- ☐ **tour de force** (tor' duh fors') [Fr.] a feat requiring great virtuosity or strength
- ☐ **verboten** (fer-boh'ten) [Ger.] forbidden
- ☐ **voilà** (vwah-lah') [Fr.] behold!

Draw a picture of the solution to the problem. Were you satisfied with the way the author handled it? Why? Why not?

_____

_____

_____

_____

_____

_____

_____

On the front cover of the flip book, write the title of the book you are reviewing, the author's name, and your name.

STORY ELEMENTS
BOOK REPORT

ANTAGONIST Who is the adversary of the main character?	**PROBLEM** What is the main complication in the story?	**SOLUTION** How is the major problem solved?
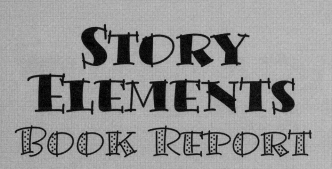		
Along came a spider	*and sat down beside her*	*and frightened Miss Muffet away.*

1. Six Basic Elements

PROTAGONIST Who is the story about?	**SETTING** Where does it take place?	**PLOT** What action takes place?
	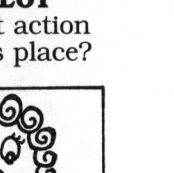	
Little Miss Muffet	*sat on a tuffet*	*eating her curds and whey.*

 In the space below, write six adjectives that describe the protagonist of the story you read.

Write a review of the book. What did you like about it? What did you dislike? Why?

_____

_____

_____

_____

_____

_____

_____

_____

_____

_____

_____

_____

_____

Describe two ways this problem could have been solved (other than the way it was solved in the story). How would these solutions have affected the story's ending?

SOLUTION 1: _____

_____

_____

_____

_____

SOLUTION 2: _____

_____

_____

_____

_____

_____

7. Solution

6. Problem

 Draw a picture of the main problem in the story, and write a couple of sentences that accurately describe the problem.

 In the space below, draw a picture of the antagonist. Around the picture, write six adjectives that best describe the antagonist.

_____

_____

_____

_____

_____

_____

Write a sentence that describes the way in which the protagonist is most like you.

_____

_____

_____

What quality does the protagonist have that you wish you had? Why?

_____

_____

_____

Draw a picture of the story's setting.

2. Protagonist

3. Setting

In the space below, write ten nouns that could be found in the main setting of the story.

In the space below, write ten action verbs that describe things the protagonist did throughout the story.

In what way is the antagonist most like you? How so?

_____

_____

_____

_____

Of all the things that the protagonist did, which would you most like to do? Why?

_____

_____

_____

_____

What quality in yourself are you least proud of exhibiting? Why?

_____

_____

_____

_____

Which would you least like to do? Why?

_____

_____

_____

_____

5. Antagonist

4. Plot

If you yourself were a *brand-new* character in the book, what would your role be? What would you have done in the story? Would your character change the outcome of the story? What is your relationship with other characters in the story? Are you a main character or a secondary character? Use your creative-thinking skills to write yourself into the story. Write a summary of your character's role in the story.

_____

_____

_____

_____

_____

_____

_____

_____

_____

_____

_____

Copyright Date: _____

Publisher: _____

_____

Other Books by This Author:

_____

_____

WHAT A CHARACTER!

1. About the Book

Title of Book: _____

_____

Author: _____

_____

Create an e-mail address for the main character of the novel. Write it in the space below.

_____

_____

_____

_____

_____

_____

_____

_____

_____

Draw a picture of yourself in a new scene from the book.

_____

_____

_____

_____

_____

_____

_____

_____

Write a paragraph about the ways in which the main character changed throughout the course of the story.

There are many ways a character can change throughout a story:
- physically
- emotionally
- intellectually
- morally
- spiritually
- socially

Think about these elements as you consider the ways in which your character might have changed.

_____

_____

_____

_____

_____

_____

_____

Create a mailing (street) address for the character. Write it in the space below.

Look for examples of things that other characters say about the main character. Record a direct quote. Is the statement accurate? What do you think the words reveal about the main character? What do the words reveal about the speaker?

_____

_____

_____

_____

_____

_____

_____

_____

_____

_____

Eye Color: _____

Height: _____

Weight: _____

Occupation: _____

Family Members: _____

_____

_____

Friends: _____

_____

2. Contact Information

3. Vital Statistics

List the vital statistics of the character. Use information provided in the novel, or use your best judgment to complete the list.

Name:_____

Age:_____

Sex:_____

Nationality:_____

Religion:_____

Birth Date:_____

Hair Color:_____

Find examples from the novel that show actions and deeds the character performs. Beneath each example, record what you think the character's actions reveal about him or her.

Example 1:

_____

_____

_____

_____

_____

Look for examples of things that the main character says about himself or herself. Record a direct quote. Is the statement accurate? What do you think the character's own words reveal about himself/herself?

_____

_____

_____

_____

_____

_____

_____

Example 2:

_____

_____

_____

_____

_____

_____

5. Words Reveal Character

4. Actions Reveal Character

If you could interview this person, what important question would you ask?

How do you think this person would respond? Write a thoughtful answer to your question in the "words" of your subject.

Draw a picture of this person achieving his or her accomplishment.

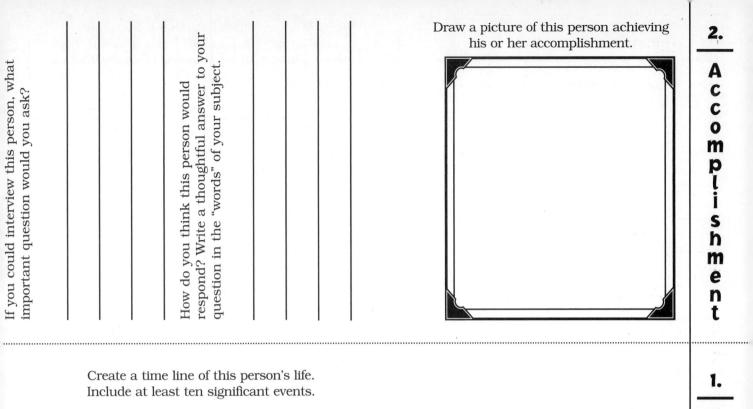

2.

Accomplishment

1.

Facts at a Glance

Create a time line of this person's life. Include at least ten significant events.

A BIOGRAPHY OF

In what ways are you most like
the person you studied?

_____

_____

_____

_____

_____

_____

What qualities does this person have
that you most admire? How could you
nurture these qualities in yourself?

_____

_____

_____

_____

_____

_____

Write a couple of sentences
describing this person's
major accomplishment.

_____

_____

_____

_____

_____

_____

Create a "Facts at a
Glance" chart on the
right that lists important
information about the
person you studied.
Include facts about his
or her birth, death,
education, marriage,
children, awards, etc.

Write the date underneath the time line.
Write a sentence describing the event above the time line.

3

Comparisons

4

Interview

5

Time Line

Personification:

to show something that is not human behaving in a human or lifelike way

Example: The mountain stood proudly in his royal white robes, surveying the realm around him.

A sentence—such as *The piano played a song*—can be personified by changing the verb to one that describes a human action, making the sentence more colorful and interesting. The personified sentence now reads: *The piano sang a song.*

Personify the following sentences by changing the words in parentheses to words that would describe a human action.

The grandfather clock (chimed) two o'clock.

_____

The floorboards (creaked) under my feet.

_____

The (chirping) birds woke me up.

_____

Circle all of the *s* sounds in the example above. (The *x* in the word exposed also produces an *s* sound.) When you're done, notice that your circles are placed at the beginnings, middles, and ends of words. On the lines below, write a sentence that uses consonance.

_____

_____

_____

1. Consonance

My Fantastic Flip Book of Figurative Language

Consonance:

the repetition of consonant sounds within a series of words

Example: The solitary mountain stood exposed, the leafless trees that speckled its slopes offering no defense from the severest of seasons.

The rain (fell) from the sky.

_____

The sun (shined) on the tiny village.

_____

John's pen (leaked) ink onto his paper.

_____

The tree (swayed) in the breeze.

_____

Rewrite one of the sentences that you personified and create a longer, more elaborate sentence like the one in the example at the top of this page.

_____

_____

_____

_____

_____

Assonance:

the repetition of vowel sounds within a series of words

Example: The clouds surrounded the mountain and anointed it with a crown of downy powder.

Circle the six "ow" sounds in the example above.

On the lines below, write a list of other words that contain the "ow" sound.

_____
(color)

look

smell

taste

sound

feel

7. Personification

6. Metaphor

Metaphor:

a figure of speech in which two dissimilar things are compared without using the words like *or* as

Example: The clouds were a wagon train lumbering across the January sky.

To help you create metaphors, think about the five senses—sight, smell, hearing, taste, and touch. If you were trying to come up with a simile for the color yellow, ask yourself—*What does yellow taste like? What does yellow smell like? What does yellow sound like?* Using these questions, you can write a poem about colors using metaphors.

> Yellow is the color a coward feels.
> Yellow is the flavor of banana peels.
> It falls from the sky on a bright
>   summer's day.
> It's the center of daisies and the
>   scent of hay.

Choose a color and write it on the top line. Think of things that color would look, smell, taste, sound, and feel like. Write your ideas in the space below. Then create a colorful poem filled with metaphors.

_____ _____

_____ _____

_____ _____

_____ _____

_____ _____

_____ _____

_____ _____

Simile:

a figure of speech in which two dissimilar things are compared by the use of like *or* as

Example: The red hues of the soil made it look like the mountain was blushing with embarrassment.

Winter is like a present that's been wrapped with snow.

Fall is as colorful as an explosion at a confetti factory.

In the space below, write a simile to describe the four seasons (remember to use *like* or *as*). The simile can be used to describe a month during the season, the weather, plant life, activities, holidays, and so on.

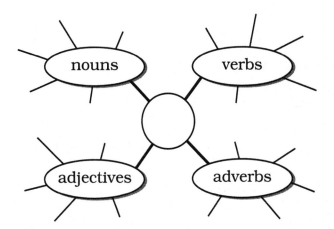

_____

_____

_____

2. Assonance

3. Alliteration

Alliteration:

the repetition of the initial sound in adjacent words or syllables

Example: Winter winds whirled in from the west, towing white, woolly clouds in their wake.

To write an alliterative sentence, it can be helpful to brainstorm related words that begin with a certain letter. Write a letter in the center circle below. List verbs, nouns, adjectives, and adverbs that begin with the letter you chose. Then, on the lines below the graphic organizer, write a sentence that contains alliteration.

Onomatopoeia:

the use of a word whose spoken sound suggests the actual sound.

Example: Whoosh! The winds cried loudly. Rrrumble! The clouds whispered in reply.

A doorbell goes *ding dong* and an air conditioner might *whirr*. In the left hand column below, list ten things found in your house that make noise. Then, in the right hand column, create a word for the sound that each might make.

_____   _____

_____   _____

_____   _____

WINTER

SPRING

SUMMER

FALL

_____   _____

_____   _____

_____   _____

_____   _____

_____   _____

_____   _____

A *tap* at the pane, the quick sharp *scratch*
And blue *spurt* of a lighted match.
—from *Meeting at Night*, Robert Browning

5. Simile

4. Onomatopoeia

Make a simple sentence more elaborate by filling in details that address the 5 Ws and How.

Target Sentence   *The cow ate grass.*

	Who	Did What	Where	When	Why	How
Target	The cow	ate grass				
Elaborated	The scrawny cow	chewed the brittle grass	near the dirt patch where the pond used to be	in the August sun	to satisfy his hungry belly	quietly
New Sentence	*The scrawny cow quietly chewed the brittle grass in the August sun near the dirt patch where the pond used to be to satisfy his hungry belly.*					

Create a word web for a word that you might overuse.

1. Word Choice

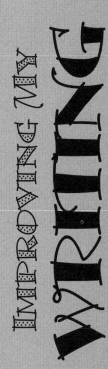

Write your name above the title on the front cover of this flip book.

IMPROVING MY
WRITING

Rid your writing of tired, overused words by using colorful synonyms. Rather than always using the word *said*, come up with different ways to show *how* someone said something.

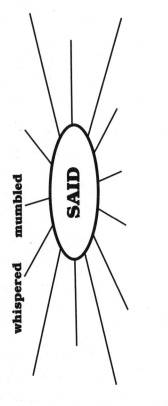

whispered   **mumbled**

SAID

When developing a character and a situation, it helps if you first brainstorm everything that person might see, hear, feel, taste, and smell in a given situation. Choose a character and create a situation (for example, the winner of the New York City marathon). Then list the sensory experiences he or she might have.

Character: _____

Situation: _____

👁	What does the character see?

(ear)	What does the character hear?
(hand)	What does the character feel (physically and emotionally)?
(mouth)	What does the character taste?
(nose)	What does the character smell?

2. Writing With the Senses

Use this graphic organizer to add detail to one of your own sentences.

Target Sentence

	Who	Did What	Where	When	Why	How
Target						
Elaborated						
New Sentence						

3. Sentence Expansion

A **shape poem** follows the outline of an object that it describes—

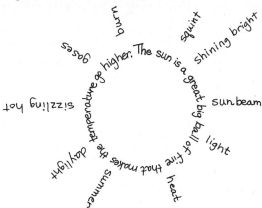

—or the words are written in a way that fills the shape of the object.

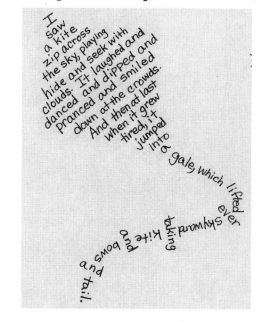

Select a topic and write your own couplet about it in the space below.

I'M A POET!
AND I KNOW IT!

1. Couplets

A **couplet** is a two-line poem that rhymes and expresses one thought. Each line usually contains the same number of syllables.

I like to watch the moon's shimmering glow,
Especially when it begins to snow.

Alphabet poems are poems that use letters of the alphabet, in sequence, to create a short poem.

Clowns
Don't
Ever
Feel
Grumpy—
HaHaHa!!!

Create your own shape poem in the space below.

Write your own limerick in the space below. Draw a picture to illustrate it.

A **limerick** is a funny verse of five lines. Lines 1, 2, and 5 rhyme and have three stressed syllables. Lines 3 and 4 rhyme and have two stressed syllables.

There once was a young boy named Jake

Who wanted to fish at the lake.

Using worms for his bait,

The fishing was great,

And soon he caught all he could take.

Write an alphabet poem using at least five sequential letters of the alphabet and a poem using the letters in your name.

A **cinquain** is a five-line poem that does not rhyme.

SYLLABLE CINQUAIN

Line 1	—	two syllables
Line 2	—	four syllables
Line 3	—	six syllables
Line 4	—	eight syllables
Line 5	—	two syllables

WORD CINQUAIN

Line 1	—	one word (title)
Line 2	—	two words (description)
Line 3	—	three words (actions)
Line 4	—	four words (feelings)
Line 5	—	one word (description)

Follow the rules to write your own haiku below.

2. Alphabet Poems

3. Haiku

A **haiku** is a Japanese poem about nature that is three lines long. The first line has five syllables, the second has seven, and the third has five.

Gems of dew sparkle
on freshly spun spider webs
in the silent woods

Line 1	—	five syllables
Line 2	—	seven syllables
Line 3	—	five syllables

Write a syllable cinquain and a word cinquain in the space below.

A **quatrain** is a four-line poem with several possible rhyming patterns.

AABB—The first two lines rhyme, and the last two lines rhyme.

ABAB—The first and third lines rhyme, and the second and fourth lines rhyme.

ABCB—The second and fourth lines rhyme, but the first and third lines don't rhyme.

ABBA—The first and fourth lines rhyme, and the second and third lines rhyme.

Choose a quatrain rhyming pattern and write a quatrain below.

5. Cinquain

4. Quatrain

Write a news article about an upcoming school event, a current event in the news, or another topic of your choice. Draw a picture to accompany your article. Include a caption for the picture.

_____

_____

_____

_____

_____

_____

_____

_____

_____

_____

_____

_____

"JUST THE FACTS, MA'AM"

NEWSPAPER REPORTING

Newspaper writers use an **inverted pyramid** format for their writing, starting with the most important information. They do this so the reader gets the basic facts first. Also, if the paper is short on space, the editor can start cutting at the end of the story and not lose essential information. Read a couple of newspaper articles to study examples of this style of writing.

LEAD
most important information

BODY
additional facts

CONCLUSION
background and minor details

1. The Inverted Pyramid

Novelists and short story writers usually tell a story in chronological order, saving the most important information until the end of the story. This allows the story to build to a satisfying climax.

OPENING
background and minor details

PLOT
additional facts

CLIMAX
most important information

Cat Hatches Eggs for Sick Chicken

7 Reasons to Go to College

City Hall Struck by Lightning

A **headline** needs to catch a reader's attention and make him or her want to read the rest of the article. It should summarize the main idea of the story in a simple, honest way. Look through a local or national newspaper for examples.

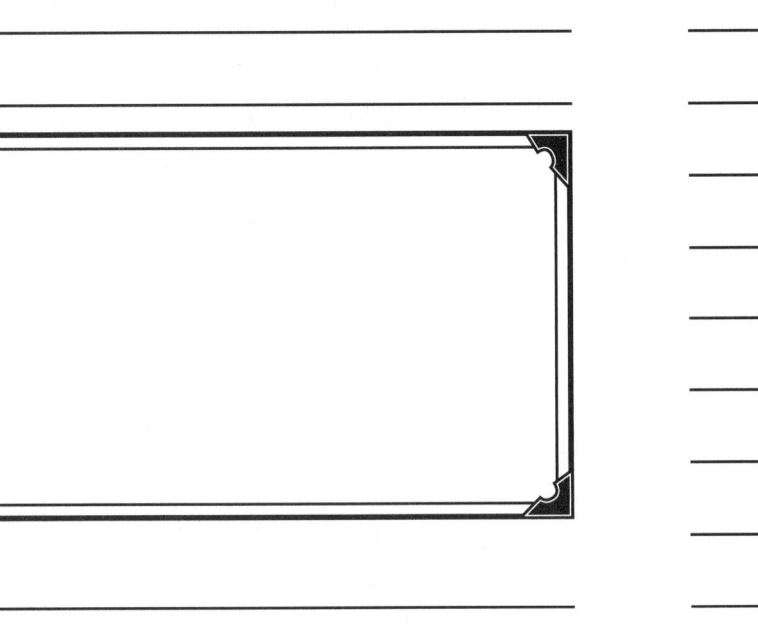

7. Reporting

6. Interviewing

Interview a grandparent or older relative about a life-changing experience he or she lived through. Gather details and facts related to the 5Ws. Write an article about his or her experience.

_____

_____

_____

_____

_____

_____

_____

_____

_____

_____

_____

Write a headline about something interesting that happened to you.

_____

_____

Write a headline about an upcoming school event.

_____

_____

2. Headlines That POP!

Read any news article and you'll find that it addresses the 5Ws—Who, What, Where, When, and Why—usually in the first couple of paragraphs.

Find an article in your local newspaper and read it carefully. Use it to answer the following questions:

WHO: Who is the article about? List names, occupations, ages, appearance, etc.

_____

_____

WHAT: In one or two sentences, summarize the main idea of what happened.

_____

_____

_____

Create an attention-grabbing caption for this picture.

_____

_____

_____

3. Catchy Captions

A **caption**, like a headline, should generate interest in reading the article. When writing a caption, don't simply describe what's happening in the picture. Include information that supports the story and elaborates on the photograph.

- Remember to identify the main people in the photograph. Put the order in which they're identified in parentheses. For example: *(left to right) Michael, Stephen, and Mela.*

- A quote from one of the people in the photo can be an effective way to draw in the reader.

- If the photo is historic, include the date that it was taken.

- Whenever possible use present tense verbs to give the photo a sense of immediacy.

- Use conversational language, but avoid clichés.

WHERE: Where does the story take place? List the country, city, state, location, etc. What can be seen in such a setting?

_____

_____

_____

WHEN: List the date, time of day, season, or other time-related information.

_____

_____

_____

WHY: Why did this event occur? What were its causes and effects?

_____

_____

_____

The First Amendment guarantees that "Congress shall make no law . . . abridging the freedom of speech, or the press." What does this mean to you? What are its benefits? What are its drawbacks?

_____

_____

_____

_____

_____

_____

_____

Should we have *complete* freedom of the press? Why or why not?

_____

_____

_____

_____

_____

_____

5. The 5 Ws

4. Freedom of the Press

Use the proofreading marks on panel 2 and correct the following paragraph. You should find 23 mistakes.

Last saturday was a very windy day My brother and I

decided to go out side and fly the knew kite we just got

from our grandmother. Paul held the string and started

running. I followed behind him, Holding the kitehigh

above my head. suddenly the kite lifted and rose higher

and higher into the the sky.

Whoosh A gust of wind tugged at the kite. The

kites tail shook like an angry rattlesnake and the red

Fill-in Flip Books for Grammar, Vocabulary, and More Scholastic Teaching Resources, page 65

PROOFREADING CHECKLIST

- ☐ Did I spell all words correctly?
- ☐ Did I use complete sentences?
- ☐ Did I begin my sentences in different ways?
- ☐ Did I start each sentence with a capital letter?
- ☐ Did I use capital letters for all proper nouns?
- ☐ Did I use ending punctuation correctly?
- ☐ Did I use commas for words in a series (*apples, plums, and pears*)?
- ☐ Did I use commas in compound sentences?
- ☐ Did I punctuate dialogue correctly?
- ☐ Did I indent paragraphs?
- ☐ Did I use my best handwriting or typing?

1. Proofreading Checklist

Write your name above the title on the front cover of this flip book.

EDITING AND PROOFREADING
REFERENCE GUIDE

2. Proofreading Marks

Editor's Marks	Meaning	Example
≡	capitalize	this is my friend john.
/	make it lowercase	Let's go to the Store.
Sp.	misspelled word	Have you (scene) my dog?
⊙	add ending punctuation	My father is a dentist⊙
✗	delete word or punctuation mark	The dog's chased the (the) cats.
⌄	add a comma	The flag's colors are red⌄ white⌄ and blue

⌄	add an apostrophe	The boys bike got dirty.
⌃⌃	add quotation marks	Surprise! the guests shouted.
∼	reverse words or letters	We don't have to go to school because it snowed night last
#	add a space	Are you going to the party?
⌒	close the space	Don't block the door way.
¶	begin a new paragraph	the park. The next day …
—	change word	We got a new dog yesterday.

3. Practice

blue, and yellow bows danced a mad jig. The kite continued

to rise until it nearly touched the clouds.

"Can I have a turn flying it? I asked.

"Sure" Said Paul, as he handed me the spool of string.

Just as I touched the spool, a suden gust pulled the

kite, yanking the spool form our hands. The wind dragged

the spool along the ground. we chased after it, but the string

ran out and lifted with the rising kite.

Paul and I stood there, watching our precious colorful kite

become a small dot in the sky, finally disappearing for ever.

PROOFREADING TIPS
- Proofread a paper several times, never just once. Reread the paper after having put it aside for some time.
- Proofread backwards, word by word. This helps you catch spelling errors, because you will be reading out of context.
- Proofread backwards, sentence by sentence. This helps you catch errors in punctuation and usage.
- Read your words out loud to help you "hear" problems.
- Have a friend proofread your paper. He or she may find something confusing that you'll need to clarify.
- Look at the verbs. Can any of them be more vivid?
- Look at the nouns. Can you use adjectives to make them more colorful?

What do you think the author wants you to take away from the book? What is the author trying to say? What is the book's theme? Use examples from the text to show why you think as you do. Include the page number for any passages you cite.

_____

_____

_____

_____

_____

_____

_____

_____

_____

_____

_____

READING RESPONSE LOG

1. Visualization

Illustrate a favorite scene from the book and describe what you liked about it.

_____
_____
_____

_____

_____
_____
_____
_____
_____
_____
_____
_____
_____
_____

What are your impressions of the section you just read? What did it make you think about? How did it make you feel?

_____
_____
_____
_____

Choose an event from the story and describe how it reminds you of something that happened in your own life.

_____
_____
_____
_____
_____
_____
_____
_____
_____

7. Interpretation

6. Connection

Use the Venn diagram to compare ways in which you and a character from the story are similar and different. (Write the character's name in the top circle and your name in the bottom circle.)

_____

_____

_____

_____

_____

_____

What words or phrases from the book did you find interesting? What did you like about them?

_____

_____

_____

_____

_____

_____

_____

_____

_____

_____

After reading the chapter, answer the following questions. In what ways were your predictions correct? How were they different? Did you like where the author took the story?

_____

_____

_____

_____

_____

_____

2. Emotional Response

3. Prediction

What do you predict will happen in the
next chapter?

_____

_____

_____

_____

_____

_____

List unfamiliar words below and write
their definitions.

_____

_____

_____

_____

_____

_____

_____

_____

5. Language

Write a thoughtful and fully developed
response that begins with the phrase:
*If I were [name of character] at this point,
I would . . .*

_____

_____

_____

_____

_____

_____

_____

_____

_____

_____

_____

_____

_____

_____

_____

4. Inference

If you could send a note to yourself five years in the past, what would you tell your younger self? Write the note below.

_____

_____

_____

_____

_____

_____

_____

_____

_____

_____

What is your favorite sound? Why?

_____

_____

_____

_____

_____

1. My Favorite Things

MY WEEKLY JOURNAL

What is your favorite word? Why?

_____

_____

_____

_____

If you could send a note to yourself five years in the future, what would you tell your future self? Write the note below.

_____

_____

_____

_____

_____

_____

_____

_____

_____

_____

_____

Write a list of ways your life would change if you could never watch television again.

_____

_____

_____

_____

_____

_____

_____

_____

_____

_____

_____

_____

_____

_____

7. Time Traveling

6. Working Backwards

Write a short story where the last sentence has somebody screaming, *"Get that thing away from me!"*

_____

_____

_____

_____

_____

_____

_____

_____

_____

_____

_____

_____

_____

_____

_____

_____

2. No More Television?!

When writing directions, it is important to write the steps clearly. Write the directions for performing a task of your choosing. Use words like *first, next, then,* and *finally* to guide the reader through the steps.

_____

_____

_____

_____

_____

_____

_____

_____

_____

_____

_____

_____

_____

_____

_____

3. The Mighty Pen

Write a short essay that explains the meaning of this famous quote from Edward Bulwer-Lytton:

"The pen is mightier than the sword."

_____

_____

_____

_____

_____

_____

_____

_____

_____

_____

_____

_____

_____

_____

What is your earliest vivid memory? Describe it in detail.

_____

_____

_____

_____

_____

_____

_____

_____

_____

_____

_____

_____

_____

_____

5. How Do You DO That?

4. Writing From Memory

MY WEEKLY JOURNAL

1.

2.

3.

ANSWER KEY

Mark My Words!—Punctuation Marks

PANEL 5:

Dear Ms. Lucker,

On May 4, 2004, we met at a conference in Des Moines, Iowa. I gave a speech on environmental awareness, and you were on the panel discussing global warming. Do you remember me**?**

I am conducting a seminar next October in Buffalo, New York, and I would like for you to be a guest speaker. Please say you'll come. You will receive a payment of $3,500 for your services, but we are unable to offer you travel expenses.

Ms. Lucker, you would be an engaging, inspiring speaker to have at our seminar. I hope you strongly consider accepting my offer. Are you available in October**?** Are you even interested**?** Boy, we sure would love for you to attend**.**

Call me at your earliest convenience.

Sincerely,
Mrs. Stephanie I. Badinger

Studying Sentences

PANEL 2:

Are you brave enough? That's what the ad said. It challenged someone to spend the night in a haunted house.

Jake dared me, "Answer the ad, Charlie." I picked up the phone and applied. And guess what? They accepted my application!

I can't believe I'm going to do this! My bags are packed, and the taxi is waiting.

Will I make it through the night?

PANEL 4:

1. garden; 2. piano; 3. island; 4. Nobody;
5. father; 6. dog; 7. girl; 8. houses
Answer to riddle: dinosore

PANEL 5:

1. plays; 2. marched; 3. scored;
4. announced; 5. cheered; 6. praised;
7. transported; 8. slept

My Flip Book of Nouns

PANEL 1:

On Tuesday, our class took a trip to the Metropolitan Museum of Art in New York City. We saw artwork and sculptures by many artists. I really liked the paintings by Pablo Picasso because he used bright colors and interesting shapes. After three hours of walking through the museum, we ate lunch in the cafeteria. Then we got on the bus and returned to school. What a fun day!

PANEL 2:

Saturday, **A**nne, **M**r., **B**ojangles, **S**mith's, **G**rocery, **M**arigold, **D**rive, **D**octor, **L**ing, **M**ayor, **A**ndrew, **L**und, **M**onday, **M**r., **B**ojangles, **D**octor, **L**ing, **A**nne, **M**r., **B**ojangles, **A**nne

PANEL 3:

1. teachers, girls; 2. bushes, benches, dresses, foxes; 3. babies, countries;
4. monkeys, boys; 5. knives, wolves;
6. children, feet, women, geese; 7. moose, salmon, deer, sheep

Don't Be Tense—Working With Verbs

PANEL 1:

1. brought; 2. went; 3. flew; 4. ate;
5. caught; 6. dove; 7. wore; 8. did
Answer to riddle: releaved

Writing With Adverbs

PANEL 5:

"It's time to go to the cemetery," Tom said gravely.

"The house is on fire!" yelled Tom alarmingly.

"I like to go camping," Tom said intently.

"I'm so embarrassed," Tom said readily.

"The earth is *not* flat," Tom said roundly.

"I have absolutely no idea," Tom said thoughtlessly.

Synonyms and Antonyms

PANEL 5:

thaw—freeze; above—beneath; professional—amateur; ignite—extinguish; yell—whisper

merrily—joyfully; gentle—tender; money—cash; difficult—hard; ask—inquire

Homophones—
Witch Word Is Write?

PANEL 2:

A flea and a fly in a flue
Were imprisoned, so what could they do?
    Said the flea "Let us fly!"
    Said the fly, "Let us flee!"
So they flew through a flaw in the flue.

PANEL 3:

Whether the weather is cold
Or whether the weather is hot,
We'll be together whatever the weather,
Whether we like it or not.

1. hair; 2. bear; 3. sense; 4. knight; 5. whey;
6. vain; 7. fowl; 8. ball; 9. their, to

Studying Idioms—A Flip Book of the
Five Senses

PANEL 2:

5. young, inexperienced, and immature
3. children often hear and understand a lot
    more than people give them credit for
1. eager to listen; sharply attentive
4. to create something valuable or beautiful
    out of something worthless or ugly
2. to pay attention and become well-informed

PANEL 3:

1. pay through the nose
2. look down your nose at someone
3. make it by a nose
4. smell a rat
5. follow your nose

Editing and Proofreading—
Reference Guide

PANEL 5:

¶Last saturday was a very windy day. My brother and I decided to go out side and fly the knew kite we just got from our grandmother. Paul held the string and started running. I followed behind him, Holding the kite high above my head. suddenly the kite lifted and rose higher and higher into the the sky.

Whoosh! A gust of wind tugged at the kite. The kite's tail shook like an angry rattlesnake, and the red blue, and yellow bows danced a mad jig. The kite continued to rise until it nearly touched the clouds.

"Can I have a turn flying it?" I asked.

"Sure" Said Paul, as he handed me the spool of string.

Just as I touched the spool, a Sp. suden gust pulled the kite, yanking the spool form our hands. The wind dragged the spool along the ground. we chased after it, but the string ran out and lifted with the rising kite.

¶Paul and I stood there, watching our precious, colorful kite become a small dot in the sky, finally disappearing for ever.